HYDROPONICS

FOR BEGINNERS

The Ultimate Guide for Beginners to
Start Your Own Greenhouse Gardening.
Discover The Secrets How to Start
Growing Fresh Vegetables, Organic
Fruits and Herbs

Larry Newman

Table of Contents

Introduction

Hydroponics can be described by simply saying that is a process of growing plants with water and nutrients without the use of soil. The water is given to the roots of the plants that are being grown. The plant roots may hang in the nutrient solution, misted, enclosed inside of a container, or a trough that is filled with a soil substitute. The substitute can consist of materials like sand, perlite, sawdust, pebbles, wood chips, or rockwool. Any substitute being used will need to provide great water holding capabilities yet be porous enough for gas exchange. Between watering the plants, it will become a storage area for water and nutrients for the root system. The plant roots grow in the substitute in order to secure the plant inside the container or the trough.

Water is the essential ingredient of all life, and it has an especially vital role in the life of plants. Unfortunately, the soil and environment that plants generally grow in are far from perfect. Therefore, the goal with hydroponics is to try to replicate what occurs in a perfectly natural and optimal growing setting. This is achieved by consistently enriching the water with nutrients, and then making these available for absorption by our plants. We refer to this water as a balanced 'nutrient solution.'

The nutrient solution that you will supply is generally provided through a human-made embedded system. This gives rise to the benefit of avoiding the evaporation that occurs in soil. In other words, we're ensuring that this nutrient-rich water is always available to our plants when they require it. Whether you know it or not, you've likely already practiced simple hydroponics by putting flowers in a vase and adding a ready-made nutrient solution.

Hydroponics is consistently growing in popularity in the modern world, from backyard ventures to hydroponic applications on space stations! Hydroponics will play a key role in being able to provide nutrition as humans continue to explore the possibility of living on other planets. On a more fundamental level, hydroponics offers an affordable means of producing food for low-income areas of the world and the popularity of growing hydroponically as a hobby has gained a fair deal of popularity over recent decades.

A great way to describe hydroponic gardening is to say that it is a soil-free type of gardening. Great leaps in technology have allowed plants to grow without soil. However, this unique way of planting that is rapidly becoming popular has been around for decades.

This is the Hanging Gardens of Babylon. These early forms of hydroponic gardening were placed on top of ziggurats, which were watered through dividing channels, and supplied with water from the Euphrates River.

Ancient Mexico also had its version of hydroponic gardening. Floating gardens, or chinampas, are gardens with plants grown in a lake in ancient Mexico.

However, the ultimate origin of hydroponic gardening occurs in nature itself. No human interference or structures took place in this naturally produced hydroponic garden.

For example, orchids are the most significant examples of hydroponic gardening. They have aerial roots that innately do not need soil to thrive. Hydroponics is seen as the next step in the evolution of agriculture by many experts as it has revolutionized the ability to grow plants and crops. It is most often used in greenhouses to experiment with and grow different varieties of plants. Hydroponics is revolutionary because it eliminates the need for what was considered a major element for growing plants and crops, namely soil.

There are three components that plants require to grow correctly i.e., water, air (oxygen and carbon dioxide), and soil.

The principle behind hydroponics is that soil provides the mineral nutrients required by plants as well as the solid medium in which they "anchor" their roots. However, it has been discovered that plants can absorb the minerals and nutrients required for proper growth from liquid medium and solutions.

Hydroponics is becoming a widely accepted technique for growing healthy and nutritious vegetables, fruits, and flowers both indoor and outdoor. It also provides us the most robust crops containing the highest number of vitamins, minerals, and nutrients and that too in a minimum space. Today, many farmers worldwide are using hydroponics for producing fruits, vegetables, and flowers because of the technique's ability to produce rich nutrients and minerals and high yields. Many farmers are claiming that their production capacity has increased many-fold after using hydroponic

The Basics: What is a hydroponic system?

There are many different methods of delivering water to the root of the plant. For the growth inside containers, each of the plants will need to be provided with an emitter for the water from an irrigation system. Water can be channeled to a row of plants inside of a trough like the nutrient film method. A large tray of specific plants can be watered from blow by filling the tray with water, and then allowing it to drain all of the excess water. This is called flood irrigation. Water is then recycled within the nutrient film method and flood systems. It is harder to recycle using a drip irrigation system and it requires extra equipment like water sterilizer and fertilizer monitoring, as well as adjustment equipment.

In combination with a greenhouse, hydroponics is a technology and is inexpensive. Hydroponics does not require a lot of knowledge and can be done with the most basic information; however, it can be done a much larger scale. It will depend on the land you have available and the time. It will also depend on the purpose. For example, a person only wanting to grow herbs will have much less work than one who wants to grow a years' worth of vegetables for a family of five. Since the regulating of the aerial and the root environment is crucial, hydroponics is usual performed inside of a shelter. The enclosures are used to offer control over air and root temperatures, light, water, nutrition, and the climate.

There are different types of controlled environments. Each component of the environment agriculture, also called CEA, is equally crucial to the process. Not every hydroponic system is cost effective. If attention is not balanced from the structure to the environment, the system will prove to be less productive than have planned. Therefore, it is extremely important to pay equal attention to every aspect of the hydroponic system.

Here is a list of benefits of hydroponic systems:

Offers the ability to produce higher yields than soil-based agriculture.

Allows food to grow anywhere that does not support soil crops.

Overcome seasonal limitations.

They are portable.

Harvesting is extremely easy.

Eliminates the need for pesticides.

Is a learning and fun experience that the whole family can be involved in.

Hydroponically grown plants like basil, lettuce, and other plants can be packaged and given or sold while they are still alive, which prolongs their shelf life.

Solution hydroponics does not require any disposal of solids.

Hydroponics will allow a greater control over the plant root zone.

Hydroponics is often the best way to produce a crop method in different remote areas that do not have suitable soil.

Solution hydroponics offers visible roots.

They are great for teaching, as well as research.

Solution hydroponics keeps your plants safe from soil-based plant diseases.

You will not have to deal with weeds.

The crops are not contaminated by the soil.

They cost less than soil-based gardens.

Plants tend to be healthy and grow larger, as well as faster.

Temperature fluctuations, over or under watering, wind damage, lack of light, and excess sunlight can be controlled.

Shade cloth is easy to install and removed.

It is flexible. You can do it as a hobby or professionally.

Seeds and Seedlings

Seedlings that are transferred to a hydroponic system grow inside the channel and can be grown with the roots exposed or even in root cubes. It is the very best way to grow them using a water culture system. Sow your seeds in quartz sand, cellulose fiber, vermiculite, or perlite. These cubes will offer weight and help support your plant. Offer water to your seeds and then cover them with paper towels or cheesecloth that is wet until they germinate. You will then need to remove the covering and thin your plants. Moisten them using a solution that is infused with the right amount of hydrogen peroxide, rather than just water.

Tips for Beginners

Growing plants using hydroponics is a huge step for many individuals and can be a large learning curve. In order to help you, here are signs of deficiencies in order to catch them before your plants cannot recover.

There is no dispute, however, between organic gardening and hydroponics. In organic gardening, however, the difference is that it is the soil that is fed with dead plant and animal matter, not the plant. Soil acts as a natural fertilizer factory that works with its soil bacteria in league with weathering to operate on those organic substances. It breaks down these substances into their inorganic composites (chemicals, if you like), so they can be fed upon by the plants. There is no soil in hydroponics, and the plants are fed directly with the same minerals to produce healthy organic soil. The plant doesn't know if its mineral food was made by man or nature or a particular care pattern. However, it does care that it is well fed, and a nitrate is a nitrate, whether it comes from a solution to the nutrient or a dead mouse.

To grow, a plant utilizes two basic processes. The first, osmosis takes over the roots from water and minerals. The second, photosynthesis, turns the water and minerals into plant tissue using light and the environment. To breathe, roots also need oxygen, and this is one of the reasons that hydroponics functions so well. The loose, chunky growing medium hydroponic, the aggregate, as it's called, allows plenty of air to reach the roots. Natural soil, on the other hand, often requires much work and time to ensure satisfactory aeration.

SYMPTOMS   DEFICIENCY

The entire plant is light green. The lower leaves are turning yellow. The growth seems to be stunted.

          Nitrogen

The entire plant is almost a bluish, green color. It may develop a red or even purplish cast. The lower leaves might be yellow. They dry to a greenish, brown to black. The growth may be stunted. Phosphorous

The plant leaves may be a papery appearance. The dead areas are present along the edges of leaves. The growth might be stunted.   Potassium

The lower plant leaves will turn yellow at the tips and the margin between the veins. The lower leaves may be wilting. Magnesium

The young stems and the new plant leaves die.

Calcium

The leaf tissue between the plant veins is lighter in color. It may be yellowed and papery.   Zinc

The leaf tissue will appear yellow and the veins will still be green   Iron

The plant's leaf's will be dark green or blue around the edges. The leaf edges will curl upward. Young leaves will wilt.   Copper

The young leaves will turn pale green and the older leaves will stay green. The plant will be stunted.

Sulfur

The growth will be stunted. The lower leaves will have a checkered pattern of green and yellow.

Manganese

The leaves will be stunted, a pale green, and they will be malformed.   Molybdenum

The young leaves will be scorched at the ends and the margins.   Boron

Note: In order to fix the deficiency, you will need to mix up a solution in a spritzing bottle. You will need to offer the solution to the plant on a consistent basis until there is a balance. In some cases, it may be best to switch the type of hydroponic fertilizer that you are using. Make sure to watch your plants to catch the deficiencies early so that you can keep them alive and ensure that they thrive.

The Hardness Of The Water And Its Compositions

The pH of a solution is the relative number of hydronium ions contained therein. The pH level varies from 0 to 14, with a pH of 7 being neutral, 0 being highly acidic and 14 being extremely alkaline (or fundamental). In this case, however, a solution with a pH of 7.1 to 14 has a higher concentration of OH-ions, resulting in it being alkaline, or basic. The pH in any nutrient solution is highly critical, as it controls the plant's availability of elementary salts. Nutrient deficiencies can occur at pH levels outside the standard due to their non-disponibility to the plant.

Water pH level Testing

Since the nutrients are administered through a water solution, it is easier to measure, monitor and adjust your solution's pH levels in comparison to when applying fertilizer to the soil directly in rural farming.

pH meter

pH is a measure of how acidic or how alkaline water is. A pH of 7 is neutral. pH levels that range from 1 to 6 are acidic, and levels from 8 to 14 are considered alkaline or basic.

Different plants have their preferences regarding pH levels. To ensure the best possible growth, you need to have a way of testing and then adjusting the pH level of your water.

For example:

Cabbage likes pH levels of 7.5

Tomatoes like a pH of 6-6.5

Sweet potatoes like a pH of 5.2-6

Peppers like a pH of 5.5-7

Lettuce and broccoli like a pH of 6-7

A pH meter can be obtained from local hydroponics stores or online. You need to calibrate the sensor with the calibration powder that comes with the meter. A basic pH meter will cost you $10 to $20.

A basic pH meter

Don't use paper test strips for the water because they are inaccurate. Most of the time, a pH meter is offered in combination with a TDS or EC meter, which we will talk about next.

TDS meter

TDS stands for total dissolved salts. You may hear some hydroponics growers referring to the TDS and not EC. These are both used to determine the strength of your hydroponic solution. If you buy a TDS meter, there will also be an option to switch to EC readings.

EC meter

Electrical conductivity is a measurement of how easily electricity passes through the water, the higher the ion content, the better it is at conducting electricity. All water has ions in it. When you add nutrients to the water, you are increasing the ion content, effectively increasing the electrical conductivity.

EC or Electrical Conductivity is an integral part of the hydroponics equation. The simplest way of explaining this is as a guide to salts dissolved in water. Its unit is siemens per meter, but in hydroponics, we use millisiemens per meter.

In short, the higher the number of salts in the water, the higher the conductivity. Water that has no salt (distilled water) will have zero conductivity.

Lettuce likes an EC of 1.2 (or 1.2 millisiemens), while basil likes an EC of 2.

A $15 TDS & EC meter from amazon

That is why it is so important to know your EC and what your plants prefer, it will help you to ensure your system is at the right level.

However, electrical conductivity needs are also affected by the weather. When it is hot, the plants evaporate more water. That is why you need to decrease the EC in hot summer months. In colder winter months, you need to increase the EC.

In warm weather, you need to decrease the EC.

In cold weather, you need to increase the EC.

An EC meter doesn't tell you the specific amount of which mineral or fertilizer is in the water. If you only use a nutrient solution using the right ratios, you shouldn't worry.

Just because it doesn't monitor individual nutrients, doesn't mean it's not useful. Salt levels that are too high will damage your plants.

You generally need to keep them between 0.8 and 1.2 for leafy greens and between 2 and 3.5 for fruiting crops like tomatoes. The source of the water can influence the EC reading. More on this later.

Sometimes, you see the recommended nutrient levels listed as CF. CF is the conductivity factor. This is like EC, used in Europe. If you multiply EC by ten, you will become CF.

For example, lettuce grows best in an EC of 0.8 to 1.2. This is a CF of 8 to 12.

The Various Types of Hydroponic Cultivation

Ultimately, you have may different options for setting up your hydroponic garden, as you will see in this chapter. We will go over several of the different methods you can use to garden hydroponically within this chapter—you will be guided through the use of deep water gardening, a common entry method. You will take a look at the ebb and flow method, as well as the nutrient film technique as two other methods that are quite similar to each other. You will see the wick and the drip systems, and finally, be introduced to the Kratky method. Hopefully, by the time you finish this chapter, you will know what you want and how you will be able to grow what you need to grow hydroponically.

Each and every one of these systems has their own pros and cons. They can each be used in different contexts and in different settings. You will be able to make sure that ultimately, you do choose the right one for you. Make sure you consider the amount of space you have available to yourself, how much money you are willing to spend, and an idea of just how involved you want to be with the entire process to determine which system will be right for you.

Deep Water Gardening

The first method to consider is known as Deepwater Culture. This particular method can also be referred to as the reservoir method. This is perhaps one of the simplest methods you can use to properly process the plants you will wish to grow. Within this system, you will have a large reservoir full of a nutrient solution you have mixed. The plants will be suspended into the solution, supported above the water, but the roots will be submerged. The roots are able to then absorb the nutrients from the solution, while the plant stays above the water and is able to get the light they need to grow.

At the bottom of the reservoir, to keep the plant from ultimately drowning in the solution by being stuck underwater, an aquarium air pump is used to ensure that plenty of oxygen gets pumped into the system. This will allow for the use of an aquarium air pump to keep the roots oxygenated as well. However, within this reservoir area in which the roots and the solution are suspended, you need to make sure that ultimately, you do not allow light into them. The light can lead to the growth of algae, and that algae then turns into other problems.

When you use this method, you are looking at all sorts of pros and cons. Let's consider a few of them:

- Pros
  - Easy to set up
  - Easy to manage
  - There are no tubes that will get clogged up
- Cons
  - The water for larger systems can get expensive
  - It is dependent upon electricity; otherwise the roots of the system may die, making it risky in areas where power is not guaranteed

Ebb and Flow Gardening

This next method is known as the ebb and flow method. These methods work by flooding and draining the system repeatedly, allowing for the system to fil the media the plants are growing in carefully, and then draining it all away. This system will flood areas at very specific intervals that are pre-programmed, and the remainder of the nutrient solution then drains back down to the bottoms. The water then pools down at the bottom to be pumped back through the system again.

This is still quite simple to use, and it is great for those plants that will require periods of dryness to properly grow in the first place. Some plants thrive in this way—they need the dryness to allow for further root growth in search of the water that is desired. However, as you have noted, then, this plant system is incredibly reliant upon a steady source of electricity and without that, it is impossible to regulate the system.

This comes with its own pros and cons as well, such as:

- Pros

o It allows plants to go through dry periods to allow them to turn out better

o It is set up to a timer, so it is mostly self-sufficient

o It recycles water instead of draining it away

- Cons

o The cons of these systems are a bit more detrimental than those of the other one. In particular, it runs an even larger risk of being destroyed by the disruption of electricity. If the electricity gets disrupted, the system no longer provides water, which can then lead to the whole system shutting down.

o The tubes can get clogged up regularly

Nutrient Film Technique

This next technique is a bit different from the others. In this particular technique, you are going to set up a long trough at a slight incline so gravity can carry the liquid down and across the top to allow for the creation of a constant flow that will go over the roots of the plants. This will then allow for the roots to grow properly and ensure they are not entirely soaked constantly. This will allow for the absorption of oxygen by the roots, which is a common concern when you consider a hydroponic setup just due to the nature of the system.

The plants benefit from these methods—they allow for the plants to get all of the nutrients they need with just part of their roots submerged. They still get the oxygen they need to ensure the roots do not drown, which is another common worry. They also allow for the plants to grow strongly with all of the benefits of hydroponics and the concentrated solution.

However, the shortcoming comes from the fact these methods usually require far more space. They require you to build a long trough if you want any effective use of these methods at all, making it harder to make good use of them if your space is limited. Beyond that, if you lose access to electricity, you no longer have that pump setup that will allow for the water to be pumped to the top of the trough to flow down. This means that while this can be a great way to grow plants, it is not always the best just due to that constant need for electricity.

Wick System

A wick system is perhaps one of the lowest costing methods you can use. When you go for this particular method, you are setting up a growing medium around the roots of the plant. This medium should be inert, meaning that it does not interact with or provide nutrients for the plants at all. It can be rocks, for example, or even cotton or wool if you wanted to use it. The roots grow within this medium, but do not require the use of the medium as well.

The wick system makes use of these items by creating some sort of wick—this could be a string of cotton or something else that is equally as absorbent, which then allows for the liquid to be absorbed up the wick and into the surrounding medium surrounding the roots. The roots are then able to absorb as much as they require. This then allows for those plants to continue to grow and develop as normally without the roots needing to be engulfed in the system. This is another great way hydroponics can be used, but ultimately, it is better for small-scale methods, such as if you were to use them at home or with young children who want to learn all about growing the plants as well.

Drip System

Drip systems work similarly to a wick, but instead of absorbing nutrients up some sort of wick, the solution is going to slowly be dripped into the system. This means you are going to require some degree of electricity to allow for the pump to work properly. You could use some slow-draining mediums ,such as peat moss, which will hold onto the fluid for quite a while before it is all able to drop out, or you can make use of a faster draining medium if that is going to better manage the setup, so long as your dripper is also properly emitting the solution.

This kind of system can be great if you do not want to leave your roots entirely submerged. However, the problem you are likely to run into with a method like this is the fact that ultimately, the minerals you are mixing into the substance you provide the plants may possibly clog up the system. If they clog up the system, you then run into the risk of your system no longer working. A clogged system cannot properly pump up nutrients and, therefore, cannot water the plants. If you do not catch this early on as soon as the problem arises, your entire system could potentially die out.

Kratky Method

Finally, the Kratky method is the last of the methods we will consider in this particular chapter. When you use the Kratky method, you are looking to grow plants above a reservoir of your nutrient solution. This will allow for the roots to then drape down to dip into the solution. This particular method is passive and can be used at home or on a wider scale than anything else that has been shown so far. Ultimately, you can use this method for just about anything.

When you use this method, you use net cups that allow for the roots to drape down toward the water, and you fill up the cup with some growth medium for yourself. This then allows you to suspend the growth cups above the reservoir of water, and the plant will grow and reach down toward the surface of the water. The plant will slowly sip away at the water, growing as it does. This particular system allows for the water to be filled up once, and then this system is left on its own to manage itself with no further intervention. This means the plants can process and grow and you do not have to do a thing.

This particular method is the most hands-off of the methods, and you can do it with small-scale operations, using just mason jars on your windowsill, or you can use large buckets. In particular, this is meant to work best for plants that will not require higher levels of water so you will not have to top it off.

How To Choose and Design The Type Of Hydroponic System For Our Needs, Calculating Space, Money And Available Time

Choosing Your Hydroponic System

At this point, you may have a pretty good idea that you wish to develop your own hydroponic setup— great! However, it is not just as simple as declaring that you are making use of one of these systems. Rather, you are going to have to decide through several different systems to figure out exactly which one is right for you. This means that you will need to figure out whether you want to spend more or less. As some general considerations that you will need to make, try keeping the following in mind:

• The money you are willing to spend: This is perhaps the most defining factor for your system that you are going to be choosing. You can spend a few dollars on a cheap setup if you do not have any supplies at all, or you could even make one for free if you happened to have the right grow medium, a bucket, some plant baskets, and the seeds already on hand. You could also choose to spend thousands of dollars on a complete setup that is fit for commercial use than anything else. Ultimately, the amount of money that you are willing or able to spend will matter immensely in being a major limiting factor for you.

• The space available: Another consideration for yourself is whether or not you are able to use more or less space. If you have an entire greenhouse that you can make use of, you can probably grow much larger systems than if you are using a spare room, or even just a corner of your living room. Some of these systems can be tiny—you could fit a small desktop aeroponic or aquaponics system just about anywhere. Some of them are large enough to grow massive amounts of watermelons. The one that you choose will ultimately depend upon how much space that you can comfortably dedicate to your system.

- The reason you are growing: Are you growing out of interest in a hobby or because you would like to try something new? You may not want to invest in a massive setup for yourself or one that is expensive if you are not sure that you will ultimately continue with the system for very long. If only using your system for a single period is likely, you are probably going to be better off with a smaller, cheaper model, and that is okay! When you use a smaller and cheaper model, you still get that full experience of being able to process your system accordingly and ensure that you can get everything that you desired. If you are going to be growing at a rate to sustain the production necessary to feed your family, you may want to use a slightly larger system, and if you want to grow enough to sustain a business, you are going to need to invest far more into the system than you would if you were just putting a small unit on your desktop. This makes sense—the more you want out of your growing, the more you are going to have to invest.

• The amount of time you want to spend on maintenance: Another important consideration for yourself is whether or not you are interested or able to spend much time maintaining your system. You are going to need to figure out if, at the end of the day, you have the time, resources, or energy to regularly check up on your system and ensure that it is running properly. If you do not have much time, you are going to want to make sure that you are using a system that is lower maintenance, and there are many of them. If you are totally fine going out and tending to your garden, you may be better off using one of the other methods that will require you to check regularly to determine how well your system is doing in the first place.

The systems that you will choose to use can vary greatly in terms of all of these points. Some of them are cheap and incredibly low maintenance. Others require you to invest at the beginning, though you should eventually see a return investment in doing so. Remember, just because you are spending money upfront does not necessarily mean that you are wasting money—and you will need to consider this. Will your return on the investment be worth it to you at the end of the day? Will you be satisfied with what you get back? If so, then great! If not, you will need to figure out another way to garden.

Now, we are going to spend some time going over several of the most common techniques that you can use when you are trying to get into the hydroponic scene. These can range greatly, and your experience with each of these, though you will require the same steps, may vary somewhat when you consider the way that you will be processing the plants, how you will monitor them, and how you will need to treat the entire process. The most common setups that you are likely to encounter early on are the wick system, the ebb and flow system, the water culture, the nutrient film technique, the drip method, and the aeroponic system. There is also such thing as an aquaponics system, which will also be briefly mentioned for consideration as well, though it is not necessarily the greatest choice for a beginner due to the fact that you will also be cultivating fish in your system as well.

Wick System

The wick system is perhaps one of the simplest techniques that you will find within the hydroponic setup. This particular method is so incredibly easy that you are likely to find it great for yourself as a beginner, or if you are trying to get children involved in the system as well.

This system is going to make use of a few distinct parts that can comprise the whole system. You are going to have the reservoir section, which will allow you to store the water within the system. Holding that water within the system is important—it means that you will be able to process and pass on that water elsewhere throughout the system. You will also have the growing tray at the top somewhere—this is where your plants are going to sit. Within the growing tray, you will need to include a growing medium—this is going to vary greatly from person to person in terms of what you would prefer. Some people find that they prefer mediums such as perlite or vermiculite while others prefer rock wool or even river rock in general. For a method like this, you will want something relatively porous so it can maintain the water content and moisture to provide it to the roots of the plant.

The third common part for this system is where it gets its name from—the wick. The wick method makes regular use of a wick that it drops down into the growing solution, routing it back up to the top of the system and filling the grow medium. The solution gravels up the wick in the same way that water travels up a pair of jeans—the material that the wick is made from must be absorbent enough to encourage the absorption of the solution to carry it where it needs to go. When that happens, the roots then get the water that they need.

Essentially, the wick will allow for the processing of everything that you need with ease. You will be able to do this to allow yourself not to worry about watering the plants at all—instead of having to concern yourself with when and where to water them, you can focus on the fact that your solution must be balanced. Due to the fact that the solution is constantly traveling up to the plant, you should be able to rest assured knowing that ultimately, your plant is going to get that moisture and nutrients that it will need.

Ebb and Flow System

The next common system that you will see used is the ebb and flow system. This is also a very basic system. However, it does require the usage of a pump to allow for the processing of the water to allow it to be pumped from one end of the system to the other. This particular system involves the intermittent pumping of the solution into the main grow tray from the reservoir. The grow tray is usually filled with some sort of grow medium that will allow the plants to root and stabilize themselves and the grow medium will then support the system to ensure that the plants that are in it will be able to get any water that is necessary.

The excess water, after flooding the grow tray, will be allowed to slowly and steadily drain down through a hole and into the reservoir again for future usage. This then allows the system to repeatedly process the same water over and over again, cutting down on waste and ensuring that the system can be kept entirely functional for a longer period of time. When you make use of this system, you are going to be required to check on it more often just due to the fact that electronic components have to be introduced—in this kind of system, the pumps are prone to getting clogged up with the nutrients if they start to coat in them, and that can lead to clogs that will then prevent the system from receiving the necessary nutrients that will help them grow.

You also run the risk that the pump will simply stop working altogether, as electronics sometimes do. When that happens, water will stop being provided to the top of the system, meaning that the plants are then at risk of drying out and ultimately dying. This can be a major problem for your system—it can mean that your system is not going to be able to survive in a pinch if you do not check on it regularly. If you are in an area where you do not have reliable power, this is not a very good method to make use of for yourself, unless you know that you can regularly check on your system as well.

However, if you do have reliable power, this can be a great option for many different plants—this system can allow you to grow plants that require periods of dryness, as some plants do. Some plants do not tolerate the constant moisture that is common with hydroponic systems, and because of that, you will run the risk of those particular plants drowning. If you wish to grow a plant that likes temporary dryness, this is a great method for you to make use of.

Water Culture

Water culture is another simple method that is essentially just suspending your plants into the nutrient mixture that you have prepared. This system is practically hands-off, but because it will require some electrical component—namely, in this case, an air pump, you will want to check on it regularly to make sure that it is still pumping and that you will be able to prevent your plants from drowning.

This system involves one large reservoir that is filled up with the grow solution that you have made or that you have bought. The reservoir is generally on the larger side with this particular system. The grow tray then floats atop the solution, usually atop the surface with the use of a Styrofoam platform or some sort of recessed table and frame that will allow you to drop plants into the system to allow them to grow. You will then allow the plants to drop their entire root systems into the water to be able to pull in the water that they need.

Because you are submerging the entirety of the roots in this particular system, you are going to find that you are best served to aerate the water. Ultimately, the vast majority of plants with root systems will not tolerate being entirely suspended in water when they are meant to be growing on soil—the roots wind up drowning because they usually absorb some degree of oxygen as well. This is mitigated through the use of an air pump that is hooked up to an air stone. When you do this, you are going to allow the air stone to sort of diffuse the water with the oxygen that is being pumped into it. The oxygen, as it rises up in the water, will naturally land on the roots as well to some degree, allowing for the transfer of oxygen to the plants to allow for them to grow accordingly.

If you are looking for a simple grow operation for at home or with children without requiring much effort, this is a great one for you. In particular, lettuce and aquatic plants such as watercress are going to thrive in this sort of system. They love the amount of oxygen that is provided by this sort of system, and if you make good use of it, you can grow more lettuce than you know what to do with. All that matters is that you ensure that you have ample aeration to the water.

If you are looking for something a bit larger-scale, this may not be the right choice for you. Many plants actually struggle in a setup like this one. Not many actually enjoy being entirely submerged, which is what you will see when you are making use of this system. Instead, you may find that another method works better, such as an ebb and flow or another system that we will talk about shortly.

Nutrient Film Technique

The nutrient film technique is another great one, but this one will require you to set up a bit more space in general to have one that is quite efficient at the end of the day. These also require more energy due to the fact that they run a pump as well to allow for the transferring of water from the reservoir to the grow tray. In particular, you are going to see that a lot of these ones will be a bit pricier due to the necessary inclusion of the pump. However, if you know that you are willing to invest, this is a great option that can help you avoid the constant soaking that you would see in the use of the water culture method.

This particular system allows the use of a reservoir that pumps the grow tray full of water. The grow tray is situated slightly at an angle to allow for the water to be run down it. Within the grow tray, you usually have the roots suspended into it. The plants themselves are typically held atop the system to allow for them to be hung over it. The water then runs over the roots, allowing just part of them to be submerged, and the problem with the roots drowning gets entirely mitigated with the use of this system. This is great—it will allow you to be able to make use of that same solution over and over again, as when it reaches the bottom of the grow tray, it then gets drained right back into the reservoir for future use. It is also a good way to balance between a system that is constantly being watered, such as a water culture method, and being able to allow for some aeration as well.

However, this system will require all sorts of interventions and maintenance. If your pump stops working at any point, you are going to struggle to ensure that your plants are properly processed in the first place. They will not get the proper amount of water, and they may very well die because of the lack of water. This is not something that you want to see happen to your plants as it would be the ultimate failure and you would have to start all over.

With that in mind, if you think that you can check on your system regularly and you have the space and money to make this one work for you, it can work incredibly well. These are quite often favored in agricultural settings, and they can be incredibly efficient, assuming that you are actually able to make proper use of the system at the end of the day.

Drip Method

The drip method works precisely as you would assume—it allows you to pump water into a steady drip through tubing to the surface of the grow tray and the grow medium. You will essentially have the grow tray hooked up to the reservoir. The reservoir will then have a water pump hooked up to it. The pump then pushes water to the top of the pump and allows it to flow straight to the tops of the plants.

Within the grow tray, you will have the plants in the growing medium of your choice—they will then slowly be saturated with the moisture, which will slowly be absorbed by the plants. This is one of the most widespread systems in terms of hydroponic agriculture just due to the way that it functions, and making good use of this system will greatly help you allow for the system to keep your plants watered regularly. If you have plants that are going to want near constant water without being suspended into it, a drip line may be a great alternative for you. These are usually programmed by you to ensure that you are always giving precisely enough water at any given time to the process.

These systems are primarily either recovery or non-recovery systems. The recovery system usually allows for the excess solution to be flooded straight back into the reservoir while the non-recovery method attempts to minimize waste by providing an exact amount of solution that you program into it. Ultimately, you will need to decide which of these will work best for you.

Additional Nutrients for Water and Your Crops

You can mix your own nutrients in large or small amounts using the formulae in this chapter. I suggest, however, that the novice start with a commercially available, premixed nutrient at least until a hydroponic sensation has been established.

In soil farming, nature does a lot of work, although often not completely, otherwise, farmers would not have to use fertilizers. Nearly all soil has nutrients in it, but you take over from nature when you grow hydroponically, and often you can improve the quality of the nutrients supplied.

Homemade Nutrients

The most common homemade nutrient is made from salts extracted from fertilizer. Such salts are available in bulk from farm companies, suppliers of plant food, some nurseries and gardening shops, and suppliers of chemicals. The only problem with this approach is that in twenty-five to fifty-pound bags, you generally have to buy some of these salts, and unless you grow in large hydroponic gardens, these amounts will make the whole thing very difficult and expensive.

The salts marked with an asterisk are the best to work with where other, identical salts are available as they have superior properties such as enhanced solubility, quality, and a lifetime of storage and stability. Of example, potassium chloride can be used instead of potassium sulphate, but if added for more than two days, the chlorine in the mix may be harmful to your plants. This is true because the chlorine in your water is likely to be in the first place. Magnesium nitrate could be substituted with magnesium sulphate but using a costlier substitute for cheap and readily available Epsom salts does not seem worthwhile. Compared to cold for ferrous sulphate, ferric citrate must be dissolved in hot water.

Besides the three essential elements of nitrogen (N), phosphorus (P) and potassium (K) for all plant growth, your nutrient will contain at least ten trace elements. The following are: sulfur, iron, manganese, zinc, copper, boron, magnesium, calcium, molybdenum, chlorine.

Hydroponics market these days has diverse plant nutrients. Their purpose is to provide the required mix of phosphorous, calcium, nitrogen, potassium, and various other trace elements to sustain growth, increase yields and allow the plant to reach its potential. Plant specifications can vary somewhat as it grows.

Concentrations and plant-food components can also vary with different growing media. The food is consumed through the plant roots and transferred to the leaves, where the plant needs energy to turn it into the sugars.

The most important thing to remember about plant nutrition is the right amounts of NPK, (Nitrogen, Phosphorous, Potassium) calcium and trace elements. The different mixes for sale may have a wide variety of ingredients.

Because the plant takes whatever it wants from the available elements and leaves the rest, the balance shifts as unused elements build up in the solution. When left unchecked, this will result in toxic salt accumulation and eventual decrease in growth followed by the death of your well-loved and nurtured plants.

This will occur if the water content is not replaced and the strength of the mixture increases. If the plant transpires 50% of the water from the storage tank, the concentration of elements within the solution is dangerously high.

The salt concentration in feeding solution is measured using an Electrical Conductivity (EC) meter. The EC meter tests solution intensity in parts per million. It means that 1000 PPM solution has 1,000 units of dissolved salts per 1,000,000 units of water.

The meter calculates total solution salt concentration and does not differentiate between say potassium salts and calcium salts. This can't tell the difference between good and bad combination, only its relative strengths.

The EC meter operates by calculating the speed at which electrons migrate through samples in a solution. In distilled water, the electrons cannot find impurities that can be used as footholds for crossing the water, so the meter returns a 0 reading in mMho or mS (these are units used to measure electrical conductivity).

When food is applied to water, the concentration of impurities in the form of salts increases, and more footholds can be found in the electrons, crossing the water faster. Thus the reading meter increases. This is, of course, a very simplified explanation, but it should help to give you the basics.

The important thing to remember is that chemical temperature plays an important part in everything. The higher the temperature, the faster the electrons, the higher the EC reading. This means you must record the PPM as mMho (mS) at a specific temperature to accurately evaluate your mixture's EC. As PPM reading is a conversion from an electrical reading and as each addition of a particular salt will change the electrical properties, you will need to use a reference solution of a known value for accurate EC reading.

Because the EC meter you use is not generally optimized for the mix used by the people who prepared your reference solution, such values may be quite inaccurate. In view of this, any reference solution that does not show the EC value in mS or give you the conversion ratio used is of no use for nutrient assessment purposes.

It is important to note that if the EC nutrient exceeds 3,000 PPM (or the meter reads over 4.0mS), the plants will begin to show signs of nutrient deficiency despite having an abundance.

The explanations for this are very complicated, but essentially because the chemicals dissolved in the solution compete for the available water, and the stronger ones block some of the weaker ones.

This leads to the roots working harder to absorb nutrients. By working harder, they have to spend more energy on production. If the temperature rises at this time and the water level decreases due to evaporation, the plants will probably die.

Probably the most important factor affecting the plant growth in relation to nutrient uptake is pH. Different plant types prefer different pH values and it is important to determine which is the optimal for the species you grow.

The medium you grow will influence the plant's cation exchange ability. This is the medium's ability to hold on-call nutrients to use plant roots. Normal soil has a high cation exchange rate (CEC) of 100-200 equivalent units.

Most rising media and water cultures have a CEC of 0. This means that once a nutrient has passed the roots, the plant cannot take it up, nor will it have any buffering effect.

Nutrients, gasses, trace elements, water and rising media all have different electrical charges and all share positive and negative charges around plant roots. This ionic combat allows the roots to consume the plant's nutrients. If the pH is wrong, the particle exchange ceases.

This is because charged particle shapes and sizes can vary from the spaces within the plant root tissue. The pH can look like a Yale lock and key. If the lock opens when the plant pH and surrounding pH vary then the lock cannot open.

Different plants require different nutrients at different growth stages. Such nutrients have different charges, so the pH must be closely monitored to get the greatest nutrient uptake. If in doubt about your plant's specifications, try to help the nutrient supplier. After all, he first made the mix and should know everything about it.

If your plants do not survive, look at the pH as the primary cause and try to find out which nutrients are not absorbed and why.

Recognize pests and diseases in time

Nutrition for hydroponics:

There are some basics of the hydroponic system, and nutrients are one of them. This section will help you understand all you need to know about applying and giving your crops the right nutrients for its survival in the system.

Since you need to meet all your plant needs, then you will have to know what you are supplying to the plant and what can be wrong if you do it too much or do not do it at all. Just as with any nutrient media, there are two things that you need to keep in your mind just as you are about to begin your hydroponic; the composition of the nutrient and the fact about all the nutrients that are supposed to contain. Secondly, you have to know what strength of this nutrient is needed for the particular crop that you are planting. This is very important as the survival of your crop is based on your understanding of this.

Composition of the nutrient solution

Several persons who grow the hydroponic system would want to buy a premixed media or nutrient solution, and this even needs to be diluted in water before use. Some of these already made nutrients usually come in 2,3 or even more parts, this is so that the grower can diversify the ratio of the mineral elements, and this can allow for a very productive vegetative growth for all the crops.

There are good brands of the already made nutrients in the market, but then you can easily have some challenges when you want to use them; this is because they have already been prepared for plants that would grow on soil hence have to be taken when you want to feed them to your plant in the hydroponic system.

However, there is a nutrient mix that is hydroponic specific, and you should get these; for the nutrient mix to be seen as complete, then they have to contain these elements. Nitrogen, phosphorus, potassium, calcium, sulfur, magnesium, manganese, copper, Iron, Boron Chlorine, Molybdate.

The concentration of these elements in your nutrient mix and then the right concentration that is best for your plant depends on the brand of the product of the nutrient mix you purchase. This is so because there is no specific recommendation for the concentrations. Some brands may also contain elements like Cobalt, Silica, Nickel, or selenium. While these are not so essential, plants can grow very well without them, yet they are quite needed for the optimum growth of many crops.

Problems with nutrients:

Whether you choose to make your nutrient solution from the different fertilizer salt or you buy an already made nutrient mix, you are also prone to encountering problems, and this usually appears as the deficiency; that is, the plant can come up with the deficiency of several nutrients. A good reason for this is a case where the nutrient is too low than the required needed concentration; the formula you are using not being balanced; some other times, growers may skip a particular nutrient salt or altogether use a wrong fertilizer when trying to weigh out the nutrient formula.

Also, even when all the factors are set right, the plant can have some internal issues that would prevent it from taking up nutrients; this can lead to deficiency and symptoms that can result.

Signs of Deficiency:

Several signs will detect deficiency when the necessary nutrients are lacking in the plants. These symptoms are quickly traced to the nutrients that are being required, and then they are supplied quickly. The growers will need to know these signs for easy detection.

A lot of these signs are quite easily detected, and they can be also similar to the other deficiency. Some of them, however, are quite distinct, but then since we are giving you quite something to worth your while, it is okay that you get the very symptoms of these, so you can easily.

Below is a list of the symptoms of deficiency for the elements that are needed by the hydroponic system for each of the elements; you should, however, note that these symptoms may be different for some crops, but this list should guide you to have an idea of what exactly the problem is.

Nitrogen;

plants that are deficient in this element are usually very short, the leaves are very pale looking and have some yellow spot colors on them. However, in the tomato crop, the leaves and the steps do not show yellow. Instead, they have a purple coloration underneath the leaves and on the stems.

Phosphorus;

Plants deficient in phosphorus have a dark green color, and also appear to be stunted; this symptom is first seen in the older leaves before the newer leaves. Also, there is a delay in the maturity of the plant. The weather can affect the uptake of nutrients by plants, and sometimes, the cold weather can be the reason why a plant show phosphorus deficiency and not necessarily because there is a lack.

Potassium:

For this element, a deficiency is suspected when the old leaves will become yellow, and then they are dark spots that are scattered around the leaves; the death of the plant soon follows this. When there is a severe deficiency, it will lead to stunted; all the leaves will be yellowed and curled. The lettuce crop will tend to appear bronze, and also this begins from the matured foliage.

Sulfur

This element is usually available, and the deficiency is not very common; there can be yellowing of leaves, and this can be seen in small and new plants grow. Magnesium; this is quite common for the tomato crop when it does occur, there can be yellowing of leaves, and this happens between the vein and which remains green.

Calcium:

Deficiency in calcium affects the older leaves, and they become distorted; they are small in size because they have spotted and dead areas of the plant. This deficiency inhibits the development of bud, and the root tips will sometimes die back. When the tip burn occurs on the lettuce plant is a case of Calcium deficiency. When the root of the tomato crop blossoms, then it is a calcium deficiency, and this is seen as a deficiency in the fruit and not in the nutrient solution. And this is a transport problem within the plant; the plant has issues with transporting calcium from the nutrient media to its fruits. Several environmental factors can cause this problem.

Iron

This deficiency is quite distinct, it is seen as the yellowing of leaves while the veins remain green; this is first observed on the new leaves and growth. It differentiates it from magnesium deficiency, which begins its yellowing from older leaves. On other crops like tomatoes, iron deficiency can be because of the cold weather and not caused because of the actual lack of nutrient media.

Chlorine

This deficiency is seen as wilted leaves, and then the leaves become yellowed, they turn to bronze color and then become necrotic. The roots of plants that have chlorine deficiency will become stunted and have thick near their tips.

Manganese; there is a beginning yellowing at the intervener leaves of the older leaves, and this depends on the plant types. The leaves get dried and brown areas, and then they begin to drop.

Boron

When plants suffer from a deficiency in boron, the size of the plant begins to reduce; the plant, as it is growing, begins to die; there is a little bit of swelling that is noticed in the root system. The leaves are then thickened, they are yellow with some spots, and then they also appeared curled.

Zinc

A deficiency in zinc will result in stunted growth of the plants and a corresponding reduction in the internode and the size of the leave. The edges of the leave may become distorted and puckered; there can also be yellow spots between the veins.

Copper

it is quite hard to get a deficiency of this element. However, young leaves will have dark green colors, and they will become twisted, with dry and brown spots

Molybdenum; this affects the older leaves majorly because they will have yellowing between their veins; it then moves to the younger leaves; the edges of the leaves will then develop cupping of leaves.

The solution to the deficiency:

Once the nutrient you use is complete and balanced, you should know that the concentration will have a primary effect on the development of the crops and plants. This is why it is essential to measure the nutrient solution using a vital unit to measure. Several growers will want to have ppm, while they still use the TDS meter, but there is an improved way of measurement, and that is the EC (electrical conductivity); this is of better accuracy and right way to measure your nutrients.

What the TDS or the PPM does is that it measures the EC of the solution, then they use the approximate conversion to put this to the PPM. The problem with this is that this kind of measurement cannot be accurate; this is because different nutrient elements will usually have varying PPM values. Hence when you use just one PPM value, you will not be able to get the accurate values of each component. The fact remains that, plants usually respond to the EC or the osmotic concentration, hence it is wiser to measure that instead of the PPM. There are lots of EC meters that are sometimes sold as CF meters; they come with the water-resistant pen meter types, and these are popularly used among growers.

Depending on your location, it is quite easy to read the measurements and then also convert from one unit to the other. The standard units used are the Microsiemens or the conductivity factor. There are also units referred to as the Millimhos, millisiemens, and the micromhos.

Here is the conversion between these;

1 millisiemen = 1 millimhos = 1000 microsiemens = 1000 millimhos = 10 CF

When you run the correct EC for a crop, you should be sure to get the right value. This is very important. Several crops such as lettuce and several other green plants will prefer a much lower EC than those of the fruiting crops such as tomatoes. Every crop has its unique EC that will aid its growth.

When a high EC is run for a plant, it's symptoms will be seen as a deficiency. A crop that is exposed to a high EC is likely to be put under stress. There is much water stress, and then the plant begins to lose water, the water in the plant begins to go back into the nutrient media. If the EC is not very severe, you may eventually see growth, which will be quite slower than the duration that was envisaged. But if the plant begins to wilt and dry up, then it means that the EC is entirely too high for the crop.

When the EC is quite lower than it supposed, then the plant will begin to take lots of water, and this can affect the greenness of the plant; the leaves become fluffy and soft and light green.

The fruit will have reduced flavor, and the quality of the harvest will be dry, and the shelf life will also be affected. Other factors affect the EC, and this includes water uptake from the solution and then making the nutrients higher during warm periods; however, the EC must be monitored and regulated frequently.

When you focus on some essential factors, which are the nutrient balance and nutrient concentration, there will be maximum growth and increased yields; as soon as things begin to go wrong, there is a need for you to identify and begin to correct them before it leads to any loss of crop. Ensure that you watch how your crops are doing so you can think of the best line of defense when you notice any deficiency.

How to begin your hydroponic farm

You have seen a lot of information about hydroponics and what it takes for you to set up one. But this section is a practical guide to how you should set up and what you should know before you set up.

You will learn how to build your hydroponic system from scratch, and basically, we are looking at how to grow plants without the soil. There are lots of reasons why you would want to grow a plant without soil. Faster growth; this is because some plant would grow faster than others when they are planted in a more convenient system. Several growers have agreed that there is at least about 20% growth speed by plants that grow on the hydroponic system.

There are other advantages like having bigger yields, having lesser hassle because you do not deal directly with the soil. It is also time-saving as the crop tends to grow faster than when it is planted in the soil. Also, the hydroponic system helps to save space and water. There are fewer occurrences of weeds, pests, and fewer occurrences of diseases.Now is a valuable time to begin the Hydroponic farm

The fact remains that the hydroponic farm is quite trendy nowadays, and it will give you much benefit if you begin to practice this kind of farming. You can start as small as the budget you have; you can begin your indoor setup by merely getting your supplies from Amazon.

In this book, there is a list of all the different types of Hydroponic system; there is the Deep Water Culture, Ebb and Flow (Flood and Drain), Wicking, Aeroponics, then the Nutrient and Film Technique. The difference between every one of these systems is just how they deliver oxygen, water, and other nutrients that you want to give to the plants.

But for this section, you will get the information about the most comfortable hydroponic setup.

Without any doubt, every expert agrees that Deep Water Culture is the easiest to set up, especially for the indoor growing system; this is because it needs the least minerals, techniques, and supplies to get started.

In the DWC system, you will have to fill up a reservoir with the nutrient media; then, you suspend the plant root in the solution; this will enable them to get a continuous oxygen nutrient and water supply.

Once you understand how it works, you will be able to maintain it because it doesn't cost too much to maintain hence an excellent choice for beginners. At this stage, you will find it challenging to get started with the hydroponics; but all you should do is to begin the traditional 5 gallons for just one plant.

As for the light, all you need to do is to ensure the plant is located in a place where it can get at least 6 hrs of light per day. With the right amount of sun, the plant can be sure to grow correctly. However, if you can't get the lights, then you will have to provide artificial lights for the plant using indoor grow lights. And just as you are starting, it is right for you to remove all sorts of factors that will seem to make it difficult for you to make progress. Hence it is recommended that you begin with a live plant instead of using seedlings. This act is known as cloning; you will have to grow your seedlings in a culture medium and then transplant to the hydroponic system.

For example, an herb, all you have to do is get an herb seedling and then remove it from the soil gently. Then you will remove all the dirt that comes with the root; if possible, you should wash it off in running water so that you do not contaminate the hydroponic setup. As soon as you have rinsed the roots of the plant, then you can put it in the net pot and lid the bucket. Once the seedling has roots already, then you can send it directly to the reservoir. This process is quite easy and would make it less tasking for you as a beginner. Cover the lid with the growing media and then allow the system to work.

Ensure your water does not kill your plants; you may consider using the reverse osmosis water as the nutrient solution because you may harm your plant. This will bring us to the fact that you need to measure the pH all the time. The range for herbs to do well in the medium is about 5.5 to 6.3.

You will only know the pH range by having a pH measuring tool. Then when you notice the pH is entirely too low or high, you will use any of the buffers to adjust it when necessary. The pH of the system can quickly get out of hand, and when it does, it can cause a lot of damage — the rate at which the plant will absorb vitamins, and other nutrients is entirely dependent on the pH.

The best nutrients you can have is the advanced nutrients. This is because they are purely designed for growing in hydroponics. They are the best nutrients to use for the proper growth of the product.

Pest prevention:

Products used to control pest infestation in Hydroponics are important but it could be risky applying pest control products when dealing with Hydroponics. Spray damages on plants grown indoors are far more rampant than we can acknowledge, mostly because we attribute these things to something else most times, without realizing that spray bottles can cause our plants harm.

Costs and Maintenance of Hydroponic System

Hydroponic gardens need to have the proper care and maintenance, or they will not produce healthy plants. Not only do they need to be constantly cleaned, but there are various maintenance checks that need to be carried out in order to make sure the system remains functioning correctly.

A faulty drain, or a leaky pipe or switch could do serious damage to a hydroponic garden as most of the systems rely on their equipment and parts to work smoothly.

Cleanliness

In order to stop the build-up of algae, mold, and fungus or to stop attracting pests, keep the growing room as clean as possible.

Equipment should be flushed and cleaned at least twice a month to maintain water levels, stop algae growth, and ensure that there are no pests lurking about the system.

In order to stop pests and various fungal growth, growers should always make sure their hands are clean. Hands should be kept washed especially after handling anything that was dirty or in contact with a harmful substance.

Do not let old fallen leaves, stems, fruit, produce or growing media or even pots or discarded trays lie around the growing areas. Rather throw out any debris or broken items, and wash and pack away any unused equipment.

Wash all equipment after use and only reuse a growing medium if it can be reused and it has been thoroughly washed and sterilized. In fact, all growing mediums, whether old or new, should be thoroughly washed before being used as not to contaminate the grow pots, grow trays, and the reservoir.

Keeping the growing area and equipment clean cuts down on the chances of infestation and development of frustrating diseases that are a nuisance to get rid of.

Nutrient Solution

The proper nutrient solution for the plant type and system type should be used at the correct ratio of solution to water.

Only use good quality nutrient solutions with an organic base. Advance nutrients are only required should there be a problem that needs to be fixed, such as a nutrient deficiency in a plant.

The nutrient solution balance should be checked on a regular basis especially is it is a recovery system where the solution is being continuously recycled.

Make sure that the solution is flushed and completely refreshed on a regular basis and that there is no salt buildup, since this is very acidic and toxic to the plants.

Watering

Watering is done in many ways and is delivered to each of the hydroponic systems differently.

Make sure the water is always fresh and checked on a regular basis. Algae is a common problem, as is nutrient build up in the system. An oxygen pump should be installed in order to ensure the water is being well hydrated and to keep the water fresher for longer.

Water solutions can come from the tap, drain systems, or rain collection tanks.

Watering can be on a continuous flow basis or set by a timer that switches on and off at different intervals during the day.

If possible, a person should always have a backup water solution available in case of an emergency and their primary watering source is unavailable. Some plants are very sensitive to their watering schedule and even a few minute's downtime and a missed watering schedule can cause some damage.

Reservoir Temperature

The water in the reservoir should be around 65 to 75 degrees Fahrenheit, which is basic room temperature. Water that is either too hot or too cold can damage the plant's root systems and their leaves.

The reservoir should be topped off with water in order to keep pH and nutrient levels constant. Change out the water on a regular basis.

Humidity

Different plants and hydroponic systems need the humidity to be on different levels. There are thermometers that can measure the humidity and temperature to ensure that the plants are comfortable. Keeping an optimum level does not encourage the growth of unwanted diseases and fungi.

Make sure plants that love the hotter temperatures get enough humidity by giving them a regular misting spray. This will help to keep the humidity constant for the plants that do not like too much humidity.

Inspect the Equipment

The equipment should be thoroughly inspected on a regular basis.

There are a lot of things that can go wrong in a hydroponic system, especially with the equipment. And the best way to troubleshoot is to try to avoid as many equipment malfunctions as possible.

The best way to inspect equipment it to keep the entire system in mind. When doing the inspection start at one point and work your way through your system.

Start with the reservoir and all the systems that are dependent on it.

- Water feeding pipe
  - This should be thoroughly checked for crimps that may not be feeding the solution correctly.
  - Nutrients build up in the pipes so they may need a thorough flushing out or replacing.
  - Check for any blockages in the pipe.
  - Check for any holes or leaks that could deter the flow of water pressure in the pipe.
  - Check for any algae or mold that may be growing in or around the pipe.
  - Determine if it may be time to replace the hoses.
  - Give them a good cleaning if they are still viable.
- Nozzles and hoses
  - Check the nozzles that feed the root systems, sprinklers, or misting systems.
  - When last were they changed?
  - Check for blockages or leakage.
  - Check any joins and washers for leaks.
  - Check for sediment build up, algae, or mold growing in or around these attachments.

- Give them a good cleaning if they are still usable.
- Drain siphons and hoses
  - Check the drainpipes for blockages
  - When last were they replaced?
  - Check for leaks.
  - Check for algae or mold growing in or around these pipes.
  - They may need to have a good cleaning as part of the system maintenance.
- Check the reservoir water pump
  - Test the pump
  - Make sure it is still working correctly and pumping the water at the optimum flow.
  - Check that all pump attachments are not leaking air.
- Check the reservoir
  - Check that there is no build-up, algae, or mold growing on the reservoir.
  - Check for any leaks.
  - Make sure the water is at the optimum temperature for the hydroponic system and plants.
  - Check that any air pumps are functioning correctly and adequately oxygenating the tank.

- o   Make sure any oxygen stones do not have unwanted algae or mold growth on them
- •   Growing trays
- o   Make sure the growing tray(s) do not have any leaks in them.
- o   Make sure the growing tray(s) are clean and have not unwanted algae or mold growing on them.
- o   Clean off any nutrient build up and make sure the trays are clean.
- o   For a closed system, the trays must be given thorough flushing out.
- •   Growing pots
- o   Check that each of the pots is still intact and not broken.
- o   Replace any that are not functioning correctly.
- o   Make sure any growing medium is clean and does not have any unwanted algae or mold growing on them that could upset the plant's natural balance.
- •   Lighting equipment
- o   Check that the bulbs are still functioning correctly.
- o   Check that the lighting is still adequate for the environment.
- o   Check the timers are working correctly.
- o   Clean any residue off the lighting system.

- Temperature
  - Make sure that any thermostat is working correctly, and that room temperature is normal.
  - Check that the humidity is correct for the growing environment.
  - Check both the temperature and humidity thermometers to ensure that they are still working correctly.
- Ventilation
  - Make sure that there is adequate ventilation in the growing room.
  - Not enough ventilation can cause mold.
  - Check that all fans and cooling systems are working correctly.
- Support Systems
  - Check that any hanging supports for the plants are working without causing the plant or system any undue stress.
  - Make sure that the environment in which the hydroponic system is housed offers the correct infrastructure for the system to function correctly.
  - Make sure the plants are all supported and planted correctly to ensure a successful infrastructure.
- Tools
  - Are all the gardening tools in working order?

o   Are they cleaned?

o   Are there any that may need to be replaced?

Look at Your Plants

Make sure you keep a vigilant check on your growing plants. Measure their growth rate, root growth and when they are ready to harvest.

This gives a person a good measure of how the next batch should perform and something by which to determine if the growing medium, solution, or systems structure may need to be changed or optimized.

The plants must also be checked to make sure they are getting enough nutrients, they are growing as they should, and there are no pests or other infestations. A lot of growing problems and deficiencies can be caused by various infestations. Some are easy to spot, others may take more of an experienced eye, but as a gardener gets to know their plants they will come to instinctively know when something is wrong.

Look for the signs in seedlings such as slow growth, looking sad and droopy, white fluffy stuff growing on the leaves, etc.

Take the time to look over the plants; do not just rush through it. If there are a lot of plants to look over, break them into sections and do a revolving sweep of one section on this day, and the next section on another.

If there is an outbreak, you will need to go through the entire growing area right away.

Spending time with the plants in a hydroponic environment can also be quite good for the mind and spirit. Plants and running water are rather therapeutic and can reduce stress, anxiety and ease tension.

Change One Thing at a Time

If you are wanting to change or expand your system, do not try and do it all at once.

Choose a section to change, switch it around, or upgrade and start with that.

Before rushing out and buying expensive parts, why not try a bit of DIY and try to make it yourself. Or at least look around to see what you have available before rushing off to spend more money on an item you do not really need.

Hydroponic systems are not only flexible and versatile in what they can grow or how they deliver their solutions, but they can also be easily adapted to suit the grower's needs and lifestyle.

There are so many great DIY ideas on how to create the perfect hydroponic garden online these days that it is well worth a try. The money you save building the system yourself can be better spent on plants, growing media, or nutrient solutions.

In order to keep a system simple and working for you, think carefully about an upgrade or addition. Plot it out and then work through one section at a time getting that part right before moving on to the next.

Greenhouse Operation

Hydroponic cultivation in a greenhouse has the added benefit that the nutrient solution is not dissolved by rain. Though greenhouses are usually used to retain plants warmer than the environment, they can also be used to regulate other environmental aspects.

The covering reduces the amount of heat loss caused by wind convective cooling and reflects any longwave radiation emitted by the crop and air (depends entirely on the cover material).

Subsequently, when the sun is above the horizon, temperatures accumulate with heat being transmitted to the soil, thereby significantly improving plant growth. A greenhouse reacts very rapidly to conditions outside, such as alterations in solar radiation levels or night-time cooling temperatures. Through ventilation, most greenhouses drop within two hours of sunset to within 1 to 2 ° C of the ambient temperature.

Greenhouses fall into these categories:

- Glasshouses: they have (at least partly) glass walls; they are very efficient, long-lasting and costly.

- Fiberglass houses: made of fiberglass sheets; cheaper, less insulated than glass houses, with a medium life expectancy.

- Core flute/solar sheet house: low cost, long lifetime (15 years plus) and more effective regulation of temperature than PVC or fiberglass houses

- PVC screen (polythene houses): made of polythene plastic, typically over a metal frame (commonly a tunnel). They are quite low cost but only last a few years before they require replacement of the cover. Insulation is worse than other safety covers.

Certain devices used in rising beds for environmental control:

- Hotbeds-Heat is generated at the bottom of a bed (box arrangement) by means of electrical heating cables, hot water or steam pipes or hot air flues. The bed must have draining outlets and be constructed from a non-rotting material (i.e. cement, stone, treated wood, etc.). Ideal dimensions are 1 m x 2 m (3 ft x 6 ft). The hotbed is packed with coarse sand or perlite extending 8-10 cm (3-4 inches) deep.

- Cold frames–A cold frame is like a hotbed unless it is heated and has a glass, plastic, fiberglass or similar cover/top material. Cold frames may be placed inside a greenhouse or outside it. A simple cold frame can be erected at a low cost and can be used to hit cutting or germinate seed (although not as efficiently as heated beds).

- Shade houses–Use to cover young plants, usually after extracting them from the spreading area and planting them in the first tub. Shade houses encourage plants to gradually ease out to the harsher outdoor world from their highly protected propagating area.

- Mist systems -A collection of mist-producing sprinklers that rain cuttings or seeds at scheduled intervals. We help to avoid drying out and to maintain the propagating plants in the leaf zone cold.

- Fogging systems-Fog systems are used as an option to the more conventional method of intermittent misting in order to provide a damp atmosphere for cuttings. The benefit of a fog system is that it still provides the damp atmosphere that is needed to prevent the cuttings from drying out and prevents the water droplets in mist systems that rest on the leaves. The lack of free water from the leaves results in reduced fungal problems, reduced leaching of nutrients from the leaves and improved propagation media aeration. Fluorescent light boxes-Many species of plants grow well under artificial light. Cool white fluorescent tubes are more desirable.

ENVIRONMENTAL CONTROLS

These are used to control what happens in the area in which the plants grow. Nevertheless, the ecosystem is incredibly complicated, and the various factors interfere with each other in several ways. For example, the amount of sunlight (solar radiation) reaching the greenhouse can influence the air temperature, or if you close a greenhouse's vents or doors, you can avoid the temperature dropping, but may alter the air gases balance.

Each time one factor is manipulated, it also tends to affect several other factors. Greenhouse management involves taking careful account of the full consequences of every action that you take.

Environment and Plant Growth The environmental factors influencing plant growth within the greenhouse are:

- Atmospheric temperature –the air.

- Root zone temperature–plants grow in soil or hydroponic water.

- Water temperature-water used for plant irrigation.

- Light conditions–shaded, dark, full light.

Atmospheric gases–plants emit oxygen but during photosynthesis suck on carbon dioxide. During respiration, plants will take in some oxygen (convert stored foods such as glucose into energy) and discharge some carbon dioxide, but the amount of carbon dioxide in the atmosphere will soon decrease in an enclosed environment.

- Air movement –gasses blend and temperatures change.

- Atmospheric moisture -humidity.

- Root zone moisture–soil or media water levels.

TEMPERATURE CONTROL

Greenhouse temperatures can be regulated in several ways:

- During the day, the sun warms the greenhouse. This effect varies depending on the time of year, daytime and the weather conditions that day. The way in which the greenhouse is built, and the materials used in building it will also affect the ability of the house to receive heat from the sun and retain the heat.

- Heaters in a house can be used to add to the heat. The heater must be able to replace heat at the same frequency at which it is lost to the outside, in order to preserve the desired temperatures.

- Vents and windows can be opened to allow cold air to flow into the greenhouse or closed to avoid warm air from escaping.

- Shade cloth can be pulled over the building to reduce the amount of energy from sunshine transferred into the greenhouse. (Greenhouse paints such as whitewash may be applied for the same impact in spring. The type of paint used is normally one that lasts for the summer but washes off with weathering to allow warming light to penetrate in winter).

- It is possible to use coolers (blowers etc.) to lower temperatures.

- It is possible to use irrigation or misting devices to reduce the temperature.

- It is possible to use exhaust fans to warm it up.

- Water storage, or rock beds, under a glasshouse floor or benches, may bridge the gap against temperature fluctuations.

- Hotbeds used to heat root zone areas will also generally help heat the greenhouse.

- Over the top of the greenhouses at night thermal blankets can be pulled, usually by means of a small hand-operated winch to capture the heat obtained during the day.

Heat loss: An important factor in the control of temperature is heat loss through the house's walls and roof. Different material forms (e.g. glass, plastic, etc.) have varying levels of heat-retaining capacity. Heat is usually quantified in British Thermal Units (BTUs)

Heating systems

Two major types of heating systems are available:

1. Centralized heating system

This is usually a boiler or boiler that generates steam or hot water to one or more greenhouse complexes in one location. Typically, this is the costliest to build and may be more costly to run. Nonetheless, there are side benefits (e.g. steam can be used to sterilize dirt, pans, etc.). This type of system is only suitable in large kindergartens or hydroponic installations.

2. Localized heating systems

Using several individual heaters, the greenhouse usually blows hot air. Hot air is often circulated through a 30-60 cm diameter plastic tube (or sleeve), which is hanged from the roof and has holes made at calibrated intervals for the circulation of warm air.

The Professional Greenhouse

What makes these glass houses "professional" level is: (a) they are made of structural steel and/or aluminum and glass rather than wood; (b) insulated glass is sometimes used, if necessary. The higher aluminum and steel rigidity than wood allows for the use of smaller parts in the building, which increases the amount of light entering plants. Registered greenhouses are almost always built on a solid concrete foundation that allows exceptions and variances in zoning to be enforced in advance in most cases.

Many of these houses are obtainable in different widths and lengths and with a selection of trimmings such as finishing posts and roll-up shutters in aluminum.

The Do-It-Yourself Greenhouse

Think about building your own greenhouse if you are handy with a hammer and have seen anything at all. You will find other proposals on the Internet by doing an internet search for "greenhouse plans." It is a job that takes only two people a weekend to finish and that can provide you with 10 or 20 years of service when using durable materials. The zoning board may need to examine the construction on your property of any type of structure, particularly if you build on a concrete slab. If an explanation or change is required, if the zoning board disagrees, the city will notify the closest neighbors. For this purpose, you should pay your neighbors a visit and fill them in on the preparations before breaking ground.

More and more businesses are catching on to the market demand for inexpensive greenhouses in a hobby-style fashion. One of those firms also built a clever line of prefabricated full-size greenhouses that UPS will send to. They snap together in a few hours from what I have heard and outlast many of their treated counterparts in wood.

For just a little beyond the time you plan on spending, lumber, glazing, and hardware, in a fraction of the time, you can get up and grow in one of those nifty prefab houses, and never worry about rotting wood and termites to boot.

SELECTING A GOOD INDOOR GROWING SPACE & SETTING UP

The room has a few key characteristics to look for when finding a good area to grow indoors. The first obvious decision is to pick a room that has more than enough space to handle your growing type of operation, the more space to work with the better. A window for ventilation purposes is one thing to look for; that will save you a lot of trouble running ventilation ducting through your building. Next, you want to try to find a space on a ground floor, so you will not get hotter temperatures as a 2nd or 3rd floor, or the usual issues of humidity that affect basements.

And a space with some sort of exposure to the water source would also be a bonus. Now once you have picked your space, you'd like to get it all set to expand your hydroponic coming in. You can start by giving a good cleaning of the room from top to bottom. The next thing you wish to do is set up your aeration. All of that depends on the place. The conventional way is to have 6 centimeters to 12 centimeters of ventilation in the vicinity of your source of light and another in the vicinity of the building for incoming fresh air. I recommend that some ducting fans be installed too, one for incoming air and one for outgoing.

Or you have a window that you can do by letting it open when the weather is nice outside, it is called a passive ventilation system. So, you always want to have at least one rotating fan throughout the room for the correct circulation of air.

Conclusion

Hydroponic gardening is the same as regular planting unless there is no mess at all. Indoor hydroponic gardening has no soil. Have you ever seen the famous Babylon Hanging Gardens? This is one of the world's Seven Wonders and is probably the earliest evidence of our indoor hydroponic gardening in human history.

Very few people now have the resources to produce something as luxuriant as this earthly wonder, but in a hydroponic greenhouse, we can grow our own minibar. It is the same as a regular greenhouse, but hydroponic because all plants are grown with water, light and air.

That is false. That is right. There is no need for soil. This is exactly what indoor hydroponic gardening is about. Growing in a hydroponic greenhouse, your favorite fruits and vegetables, is the latest fad among gardeners. Everything you need and if you really want to go to the local pond and garden shop and hydroponic packages. Or you test all the wonderful might make your own.

Recommendation to a novice, however, is to get one of the hydroponic kits. Many people use one of the two popular hydroponic kits: a hydroponic ebb and flow kit or a hydroponic deep culture Pack. These would be simple and basic hydroponic packages all your own hydroponic greenhouse needs to start. If you want to extend your hydroponic greenhouse, you will probably have to buy additional lights and more nutrient solutions. Nonetheless, it's a good investment in the long run.

Scientific studies show that hydroponic greenhouse goods are lighter, juicier, and more nutritious than store purchases. The additional bonus is that there are almost no weed issues that outdoor gardens usually face. In a hydroponic greenhouse, there are very few pests. This, in turn, means that harmful and dangerous pesticides and insecticides are not needed. Another great advantage is that you can cultivate your favorite fruit and vegetables throughout the year with hydroponic kits. Yeah! Wow! How cool this is! You could at whatever time of the year grow your food, protect your family from harmful chemicals, and enjoy your favorite foods.

Hydroponic indoor gardening is a wonderful hobby. There is practically no clutter, no additives, and many benefits can be seen in the eye. You grow a garden that you enjoy and avoid all the downsides and headaches that usually come with gardening. Go out, then, if you want to try something new. Take some of your mates, go to the store and purchase hydroponic kits and make your own hydroponic greenhouse.

Not only does hydroponics allow for fast, efficient, cost effective growing environments, but it is a means to grow produce where it otherwise was not able to grow. Thanks to innovative irrigation systems and the use of various growing media, places that have inadequate soil composition are able to grow fresh produce.

Hydroponics also provides a growing solution for places that have little to no space for commercial growing lands. It has even been successfully tested in space. Hydroponics is not a new concept but has come a long way since ancient times and keeps moving forward in leaps and bounds with new methods being introduced along the way.

It is not a hard concept to grasp and some methods are really easy to learn. There are ready-made kits that one can buy and assemble for each type of system. But they are all capable of being homemade with materials found around the home.

Hydroponics is a great way to teach children the joy of gardening without the mess of dirt and as the plants grow relatively quickly it holds their attention better than normal gardening does.